Oranges

Oranges:
All About Them

by

Alvin and Virginia Silverstein

illustrated by Shirley Chan

Prentice-Hall, Inc. Englewood Cliffs, N.J.

for Gloria and Charles Green

Text Copyright © 1975 by Alvin and Virginia B. Silverstein
Illustrations Copyright © by Prentice Hall, Inc.

Printed in the United States of America J

Prentice-Hall International, Inc., London
Prentice-Hall of Australia, Pty. Ltd., North Sydney
Prentice-Hall of Canada, Ltd., Toronto
Prentice-Hall of India Private Ltd., New Delhi
Prentice-Hall of Japan, Inc., Tokyo

Library of Congress Cataloging in Publication Data

Silverstein, Alvin.
    Oranges: all about them.

    SUMMARY: Introduces the orange in legend and
history, its growth and cultivation, and its use as
a food. Includes experiments, recipes, and games
with oranges.
    1. Orange—Juvenile literature. [1. Orange]
I. Silverstein, Virginia B., joint author. II. Title.
SB370.07S47   641.3'4'31   74–7498
ISBN 0–13–638809–4

Table of Contents

ORANGES!

In 1421 an orange seed was planted by the gardener of the Queen of Navarre. Soon a tiny shoot poked out of the soil and grew into a slender seedling with rich green leaves. The seedling grew into a tree, and after five years or so, it began to bear shining oranges. The tree was so handsome, and it bore such a profusion of oranges, that people from all over the kingdom came to the Royal Gardens to look at it. Years went by, and kings and queens reigned and died, but the orange tree lived on. Navarre was ruled at that time by a member of the Bourbon family, and eventually the prize orange tree was inherited by the northern branch of the family. In the early 1500s, the Constable of Bourbon transplanted the tree and moved it to a special building—an "orangerie"—at Chantilly . Then in 1532, the king of France,

Francois I, moved the tree again, to his new palace at Fontainebleau. The tree, more than a hundred years old, still lived and thrived and continued to bear fruit. It had a name now, several of them in fact, reflecting its long history. It was called "the Constable," or "le grand Bourbon," and sometimes "the Francois I." Kings and commoners continued to live out their lives while the old orange tree went on. Late in the seventeenth century it made another journey, when King Louis XIV built a splendid new orangerie at Versailles. There "the Constable" was a silent witness to the gaiety of royal balls, and then the violence of the Revolution, the triumphs and tragedies of the Empire, and the founding of a new Republic. Finally, in 1894, "le grand Bourbon" died at the age of four hundred and seventy-three.

It is not very likely that many more orange trees will live for nearly half a millennium. Yet there are a number of trees in Florida orange groves that are still bearing fruit after more than a century.

Orange trees are prized both for their fruit and as attractive ornamental trees. Their leaves are a rich, glossy green, and they bear a profusion of waxy white blossoms with a sweet odor. Orange blossoms are the traditional flower for bridal bouquets, and the official state flower of Florida.

Oranges, like other members of the citrus group, are warm-climate trees. They came originally from Southeast Asia, but are now grown in most of the warm regions of the world. In cooler regions they can also be grown indoors, or taken indoors for the winter.

A glass of orange juice in the morning and an orange in the lunchbox have long been a traditional part of American life. Yet oranges have a variety of other uses as well. Oils extracted from the blossoms, peels, and leaves are used in products from perfume to salad oil, and even paints and varnishes. Orangewood has been prized for fine-quality furniture for centuries. The glowing orange fruits and fragrant white blossoms of orange trees have also found their way into the legends and lore of many lands.

THE STORY
OF ORANGES

The ancient Romans believed that the first citrus fruits were brought to Italy by the Hesperides, the daughters of Atlas, who crossed the Mediterranean Sea from Africa in a giant shell. Actually, oranges and their relatives probably reached Europe after a longer and more complicated series of journeys.

THE HISTORY
OF ORANGES

Citrus trees probably first appeared in the Malay Archipelago more than twenty million years ago, before the islands of the

South Pacific had split off from the great land mass that included Asia and Australia. The first citrus plants, whose fruits were more bitter than today's oranges, spread to various parts of Asia, and in China the first of the modern forms developed. Even today, more citrus varieties can be found in China than anywhere else in the world.

From China, the junks of early seamen carried citrus seeds and trees eastward to Japan and the South Pacific, westward to India and Africa, and eventually to Italy. One of the first of the citrus trees to be spread in this way was the citron, for which the group is named.

The name "citrus," which really means "cedar," came to be applied to the oranges and their relatives as a result of a misunderstanding. The large, rough-skinned, greenish-yellow fruits of the citron look something like the cones of the cedars of Lebanon, a type of evergreen tree. The Greeks named the citron the *kedromelon*, or "cedar apple." In Latin this became *malum citreum*, or often simply *citreum*. As oranges, lemons, and other citrus fruits became established in Italy, the name was extended to all of them.

The Roman conquerors helped to spread oranges and other citrus fruits through the lands of their empire. Even more important were later Arab traders and soldiers, who left a trail of citrus trees to mark their progress. During the sixth and seventh centuries, the armies of Islam conquered a wide sweep of territory from India through northern Africa to Spain. By the tenth century, oranges were growing in all the countries of the Mediterranean region. In Moorish Spain, no unbeliever was permitted to eat an orange or drink its juice unless he first accepted the faith of the Prophet.

Crusaders returning from Saracen lands brought back stories of oranges and added to their popularity in Europe. But for some time, oranges were not usually eaten as fruits in the countries of Europe. Orange trees were prized for their beauty and for the delightful odor of the blossoms and peel. Oranges were used as a seasoning for meat and fish, and their peels were candied. But until about 1500, the oranges that were grown in Europe were mainly bitter oranges. Then Portuguese traders brought sweet orange trees back from India, and the new type swept through Europe. In many countries, the new sweet oranges were called Portugals, and they became wildly popular. In regions that were too cold for citrus trees, special "orangeries" were built. In these buildings, with many glass windows and a heated floor, orange trees were grown in large pots for their blossoms and fruit. The most famous of these orangeries was the one built in Versailles for King Louis XIV of France. It was in the shape of a C, twelve hundred feet around, and parties and balls were held there amid the sweet scent of the orange blossoms.

About a century after the Portugal Oranges were brought to Europe from India, Portuguese missionaries sent back word of a delicious new type of sweet orange growing in China. In 1635 a Chinese orange tree was sent to Lisbon, Portugal, and soon the China Oranges were the new delight of Europe.

The Spanish and Portuguese explorers carried oranges with them to the New World. Christopher Columbus planted the first orange trees in the Western Hemisphere in 1493, on his second expedition. He had brought seeds with him, and planted them on the island of Hispaniola (now Haiti). Later expeditions continued the practice; indeed, Spanish law required that each sailor on a ship bound for America carry a hundred seeds with him. Later, because the seeds tended to dry out, the ships carried young trees instead. Citrus groves sprang up around Spanish settlements in South and Central America, in Mexico and in Florida.

Indians who visited the settlements carried oranges away with them and scattered the seeds through the wilderness, and soon orange trees were growing wild.

The first mention of oranges in Florida dates back to 1579, in the settlement of St. Augustine. Oranges were probably introduced when St. Augustine was first settled, in 1565.

Oranges were not introduced into California until two centuries later. In 1769, the Franciscan mission fathers planted oranges at San Diego. A chain of missions was gradually built over a stretch of four hundred miles along the coast. As the Franciscans spread their faith, they also helped to spread oranges, planting groves at each mission. The oranges thrived in the sunny California climate.

In 1841 a trapper and Buffalo hunter from Kentucky, William Wolfskill, arrived in Los Angeles. He was tired of a wandering life and settled down near the sunny California town. He got some trees from the San Gabriel Mission garden and began to raise oranges and lemons. They did so well that Wolfskill expanded his plantings to seventy acres. Then, in 1849, came the great Gold Rush. Men from all over the United States rushed into California to stake their claims

for gold. Thirsty miners were delighted with the refreshing "Wolfskill oranges" and helped to spread their fame.

Another important event in the saga of California and its oranges was the building of the transcontinental railroad, which linked the west coast with the east. William Wolfskill decided to take a gamble. In 1877 he loaded an entire freight car with oranges and sent them east to St. Louis. It took the "orange car" a whole month to reach its destination. But when it was opened in St. Louis, the fruit was still in fine condition. The people of the city quickly bought the entire shipment. The following winter, when icy blizzards howled outside, some of the people who had eaten the golden "Wolfskill oranges" thought about the sunny land out west where the fruits were grown. They dreamed about leaving the dreary winter weather behind—and some of them did. In growing numbers travelers rode the new railroads out to California. Many stayed, and wrote to friends and relatives about the golden land and its golden fruits. Soon there was a new "gold rush," as Easterners sought a new life in California.

Many of the new settlers sank their life savings into orange groves, dreaming of the fortunes they would make. But an orange grove is not a very good investment for someone who wants to make a fortune in a hurry. As the young orange trees slowly grew to bearing age, years went by, and there was no income. Much of the land the eager growers bought was too cold or too dry for orange groves, and trees died. Many lost their life savings and sadly went back to their old homes. Whole towns became ghost towns.

But some of the growers determinedly stuck it out. Gradually it was found that certain orange varieties did especially well in certain parts of California. Valencia oranges, which ripened in the summer, flourished in Orange County, near Los Angeles. The

Riverside region turned out to be ideal for navel oranges, a new variety that had recently been introduced. By the late 1800s, the California orange industry was firmly established.

Meanwhile, in Florida, oranges did not really become a major crop until the territory became a United States possession in 1821. The Spanish, with their famous groves in Andalusia and Valencia, had no need to start large commercial groves in their possessions overseas. But after 1821 the Florida orange groves spread quickly. People up north heard tales of orange growers who made a comfortable living with practically no work at all, spending most of their time hunting and fishing. Soon many Northerners moved down to Florida to start orange groves of their own. Loads of oranges were shipped by boat to markets in northern cities, and the young Florida citrus industry was thriving.

But then, early in 1835, disaster struck. Though Florida winters are normally mild, on February 8 the temperature fell below freezing and then continued to plummet —as low as eleven degrees Fahrenheit—so low that even the salt water in the bays froze. Orange trees are warm-weather plants, which do not have the inborn resistance to cold that apple trees and many other trees have. As the freezing temperatures continued for more than two days, one tree after another fell victim to the frost. In three days, nearly every orange tree in Florida was dead.

One small grove survived the frost of 1835. This grove had been planted in 1830 by a young man named Douglas Dummett on Merritt Island, between Cape Canaveral and the mainland, on high ground between the Indian River and the Banana River. The warm waters surrounding the grove and the height of the land helped to protect the trees. (Cold air tends to flow downhill.) In the years that followed, buds from Dummett's grove on the Indian River helped to revive the orange groves in Florida. But this time, care was taken to choose warmer locations for the groves.

ORANGES IN LEGEND AND LORE

The modern bride, carrying the traditional bouquet of orange blossoms, probably does not know that the sweet-smelling flowers are ancient symbols. The white flowers stand for purity and everlasting love. And since the orange tree is an extremely fruitful one, the wedding orange blossoms are also a promise of fruitfulness of the marriage to come. But, so the old superstitions go, the wedding bouquet must be thrown away before it withers—otherwise, it will bring barrenness.

The tradition of using orange blossoms in a bride's bouquet was carried back to Europe from Saracen lands by returning Crusaders. From the mainland the custom was carried to England, and then to North America.

Wherever oranges have been grown, they have found their way into local legends and superstitions, usually as symbols of good fortune. In China and Japan, oranges, as fruits of the timeless tree (since an orange tree is evergreen and continues to bear year after year), were regarded as bringers of good luck and immortality. A modern echo of this belief is found in the Florida Citrus Commission promotions: Ponce de Leon, the Spanish discoverer of Florida, they say, was searching for the Fountain of Youth, but instead he brought it along with him.

In Greek and Roman mythology, "golden apples" believed to be oranges appear as a recurring theme, symbolizing a great prize or a love gift. Gaea, the ancient earth goddess, presented a golden apple to Hera as a wedding gift on the day she married Zeus, the king of the Greek gods. The seeds of this fruit were planted and grew into trees that were entrusted to the Hesperides, the daughters of Atlas. In their garden, at the western edge of the world, the serpent Ladon guarded the trees. One of the twelve labors of Hercules was to bring back the golden apples of the Hesperides.

In another myth, a young huntress named Atalanta was warned that she should not marry, for marriage would be her ruin. Atalanta discouraged her many suitors by setting a condition for winning her hand: she would marry any man who could beat her in a race, but death would be the penalty for all who tried and failed. A young man, Hippomenes, was the judge of the race, but when he saw Atalanta at the starting line, he fell in love with her himself. After the young huntress's unfortunate suitors had failed and been put to death, Hippomenes challenged her to a new contest. As they prepared for the race, Hippomenes prayed to the goddess of love, Venus, and she gave him three golden apples. During the race, each time it seemed that Atalanta was going to outrun Hippomenes, he threw a golden apple before her. As she hesitated, then stopped to pick it up, Hippomenes took the lead. Atalanta was happy to lose this race, for she had fallen in

love with Hippomenes. But the lovers were so full of their own happiness, that they forgot to show proper gratitude to Venus for her help. The goddess was angered and caused them to offend another goddess, Cybele. Cybele turned them into a lion and a lioness and yoked them to her chariot.

During the Renaissance, oranges were often used by artists as a symbol for the Holy Land. Crusaders had brought home tales of the beautiful citrus groves in Palestine, not realizing that oranges and other citrus fruits had been introduced by the Arabs many centuries after the time of Christ. (Oranges are not mentioned in the Bible.) So the great

Italian masters, thinking they were adding a particular touch of authenticity, carefully painted Christ and his followers in citrus groves and placed oranges on the table at the Last Supper. In a further confusion that arose at this time, the Virgin Mary became identified with orange blossoms. Earlier Bible scholars had traced an association with the cedars of Lebanon, so now the "cedar apples" became a symbol of the Virgin. Paintings of the Madonna and Child were set in orange groves or decorated with garlands of orange blossoms.

As oranges spread through the world, legends, superstitions, and folk remedies spread with them. Boccaccio's *Decameron*, written in the fourteenth century, was filled with mentions of orange blossom water and orange perfume. In England and Italy, oranges were used in witchcraft as a symbol for the human heart. If a witch wished to kill a victim, she wrote his name on a piece of paper, pinned it to an orange, and then placed the orange in the chimney until the victim died. Oranges were also used as love charms. In one curious practice in England, a lovesick swain was advised to prick an orange in the pits of its skin with a needle, then go to sleep with the orange tucked into his armpit. The next day, he must give it to the girl he loved and get her to eat it. If she did, she would be sure to return his love. At the same time, oranges and orange blossoms were put to a more effective use in the arts of love by making perfumes and cosmetics from them.

A twelfth-century physician in Tunis recommended orange peel preparations as cures for colic and tapeworm. In Renaissance Italy, oranges were recommended as a preventative for the plague. (One of the biggest orange boosters unfortunately died of the plague.)

A more realistic orange remedy was discovered when seafarers found that the bleeding gums, fatigue, easy bruising, and

loss of hair that they developed on long sea voyages got better almost immediately when they docked at a port where oranges and other citrus fruits were growing. We know now that sailors of old suffered from a disease called scurvy, caused by a lack of vitamin C in their normal diet of salt meat and ship's biscuit. Oranges and other citrus fruits are particularly rich in vitamin C and thus can prevent and cure scurvy. Spanish ships carried orange seeds and trees with them and planted them wherever they went in order to have a ready supply of fresh citrus fruits at each stage of their voyages. The English navy coped with the same problem by ordering daily rations of lime juice for all sailors—a practice that gained them the name of "limeys." New studies indicate that vitamin C may be helpful in preventing heart attacks, and high doses of vitamin C have been found effective in preventing the common cold. Perhaps the "fountain of youth" claims of the Florida Citrus Commission are not so fanciful after all.

THE KINDS
OF ORANGES

Around 1950, many of the Persian Lime trees in Florida fell victim to a serious virus disease. Agricultural researchers began a frantic effort to breed a virus-free strain of Persian Limes. They could not use the usual method for reproducing or propagating citrus trees, by grafting buds onto a young, sturdy, already established tree. For plant virus diseases are transmitted through the buds. The limes of the new strain would have to be grown from seeds. Yet Persian Limes are seedless fruits.

Fruits are considered seedless if they normally have fewer than five seeds. So the researchers cut up one lime after another—nearly two thousand of them—vainly looking for seeds. They went to a processing plant that produced lime concentrate and carted off two dump trucks full of pulp from tens of thousands of Persian Limes, and then sorted through the mess by hand. They found two hundred and fifty lime seeds and planted them. Seedlings grew, and the researchers raised them with care, only to find that they had sweet orange trees, bitter orange trees, grapefruit trees, lemon and tangerine and citron trees—and two Persian Lime trees.

As you might guess from this story, the different kinds of citrus trees are very closely related. Even though their fruits look and taste quite different, the pollen from flowers of one type can readily fertilize flowers of another type, producing cross-bred or hybrid plants. Such cross-breeding may be done on purpose, by researchers trying to breed new varieties with desirable qualities. The tangelo, for example, is a cross between the tangerine and the grapefruit, which was first produced in 1897 by a U.S. Department of Agriculture researcher, W. T. Swingle. Other hybrids may be formed accidentally. The Persian Lime is very likely just such a natural hybrid, and the seedling that grew from Persian Lime seeds resemble various ancestors.

Scientists generally give plants and animals Latin names, consisting of two parts, so that a scientist in one part of the world can read a paper written by a scientist in another part of the world and know exactly what kind of plant or animal he has studied, even though local names for them may vary greatly. The first part of the Latin name, called the genus, is like a person's family name, while the second part, the species, is like a person's first name. A dog, for example, is called by scientists *Canis familiaris*—*Canis* is the genus name and *familiaris* is the species name. Oranges, lemons, limes, grapefruits, citrons, kumquats, and other citrus fruits all belong to the same genus, *Citrus*, but each has its own species name. There are several different species of oranges, and within each species there are a number of varieties.

The first true oranges were probably the sour or bitter oranges, which scientists call *Citrus aurantium*. (The second part of the name comes from a root meaning golden.) As might be guessed, the fruits of these oranges have a sour and bitter taste, and are not very good for eating. The ripe fruits are a brilliant orange, with a slight reddish tint. The rough-surfaced peel is prized for making marmalades, and the orange-colored flowers are used to make fine perfumes and colognes. The bitter orange is sometimes called the Seville orange, because it was widely grown in the Seville region in Spain. In Europe it is still grown for its peel and for the essential oils that are extracted from the blossoms, buds, shoots, and leaves of the trees. But in the United States, the main use of bitter orange trees is as rootstocks, the established young trees onto which buds of other varieties are grafted. Trees budded onto bitter orange rootstocks usually bear excellent fruits. These rootstocks are hardy and resistant to cold weather, but they do not grow very well in the sandy soil that is found in many parts of Florida. In addition, they are susceptible to a disease called tristeza, which has damaged or killed many orange trees in recent years. Although bitter orange used to be the most commonly used stock, now most orange trees in Florida are budded onto rootstocks of rough lemon. (It seems strange to think of orange trees growing on lemon roots, but some even stranger unions are common in the citrus world. In fact, buds of several different kinds of citrus fruits can be grafted onto the same rootstock, and when the tree is mature, it may bear oranges, lemons, limes, grapefruits, tangerines, and kumquats all at once.)

The oranges most often used for fruit and juice today are sweet oranges, *Citrus sinensis* (the China orange). Like the sour oranges, sweet oranges came from China. In the United States they are grown in only a few states: Florida, California, Texas, Arizona, and Louisiana. Orange trees usually bloom in the spring, and then the fruit takes from eight to fifteen months to reach maturity, depending on the variety. In Florida, the orange season lasts from November to mid-June; the fresh oranges that are sold during the rest of the year come from California. Florida oranges are usually much juicier than California oranges with a thinner, tighter-fitting skin. There is a good reason for this difference—on the average, each acre of Florida orange groves receives more than a million more gallons of rain each year than a similar acre in California. California orange growers say that you have to get into the bathtub to eat a Florida orange. Florida orange men retort that if you ran over a California orange with a ten-ton truck, you wouldn't even wet the pavement.

One of the main types of sweet oranges grown in California is the navel orange. The name of this variety comes from a formation at the blossom end of the fruit that looks like a person's navel. Navel oranges are actually double fruits—the "navel" is really a small second orange that does not develop fully. This variety first appeared in 1810 as a mutation or sudden change on a single branch of an orange tree in the Bahia district of Brazil. Navel oranges are prized as eating oranges, for they are usually seedless, and they are especially easy to peel and section.

Navel oranges ripen in the fall and winter, from November to the beginning of May. Then, in the spring and summer, the California Valencia oranges ripen. These are large, smooth-skinned seedless fruits, loaded with juice. Valencia oranges originally came from Spain, but few are still grown there. In the United States, Valencia oranges are grown in all the orange-producing states. (In Florida they ripen from March to July, the end of the Florida orange season.) Valencias

are so popular that they account for about half the whole U.S. orange crop.

Florida has some sweet orange varieties all its own. Hamlins, smooth-skinned seedless oranges, and Parson Browns, pebbly-skinned oranges with a few seeds, ripen in the fall, early in the Florida season. Both varieties were named after the orange growers who first raised them. Pineapple oranges are a mid-season variety especially prized for their juicy sweetness. They are attractive fruits, with a smooth, bright-orange skin and about a dozen seeds. They were originally called Hickory oranges, but workers in orange juice factories soon renamed them for their strong pineapplelike aroma. Pineapple oranges are fine juice oranges, but they must be eaten quickly after they are picked. They do not keep as long as most other varieties, because their skin is weak and decays easily.

The blood orange is an unusual orange variety that is more popular in Europe than in the United States. Oranges get their color from orange pigments called carotenoids in the outer part of the peel. In blood oranges, red pigments called anthocyanins are also found in the juice of the fruits, giving it a reddish, "bloody" tinge.

The orange group also includes an-

other species, *Citrus reticulata*. (The second part of this name means "netted.") These are the tangerines and mandarin oranges. Smaller than sweet oranges, with a bright orange color, tangerines are noted for their loose-fitting skin, which peels down just like a zipper opening up.

Plant breeders have crossed the zipper-skinned tangerine with other citrus species to come up with valuable new varieties. Temples and Murcotts are crosses between tangerines and sweet oranges. Their easy-to-peel skin and sweet, juicy taste make them excellent oranges for eating in the hand. It has been claimed that Temple oranges come from the Orient and were grown from seeds

stolen from a Buddhist temple. But this romantic story is not true. Actually they were bred in Florida and were named for William Chase Temple, who was once general manager of the Florida Citrus Exchange.

A cross between a tangerine and a grapefruit (which scientists have named *Citrus paradisi*) produced the tangelo. It looks like a large, brightly colored orange. The tangelo's skin is the zipper skin of the tangerine, and it is as juicy as a grapefruit. Its taste is a delightful blend of the tangerine's sweetness and the grapefruit's tangy tartness. It ripens in the middle of the Florida season, from December to March.

GROWING ORANGES

The next time you eat an orange, take special note of how many seeds it has. Even in a seedless variety, you may well be able to find a few seeds. Try planting some of the seeds about half an inch deep in a pot of soil. Water the soil from time to time, keeping it moist but not wet, and wait. Nothing will happen for a while, and you may be convinced that the seeds are not going to sprout after all. But then, after three or four weeks, shoots will poke up out of the ground. Soon they will grow into sturdy seedlings with glossy green leaves.

Young orange seedlings are attractive house plants, but if you want to let them grow up to be trees, you will eventually need a lot of room and a very big pot for each. If you live in a warm region, such as Florida, California, Arizona, or Texas, you can transplant your seedling trees outside after a year or so. But orange trees, like other citrus trees, can stay outdoors only in places where the temperature does not usually go below freezing. A drop to 25°F, even for only a few hours, may cause some damage to an orange tree, while temperatures below 20°F may kill it.

In Florida, where several great freezes have nearly wiped out the citrus industry, land for orange groves is chosen with great care, to provide the best possible protection from cold. Orange groves that once flourished in more northern parts of the state have been abandoned. Sites near rivers and lakes are prized, for bodies of water tend to keep temperatures more even and protect against killing frosts. Orange groves are often planted on hills and rises, for cold air tends to flow downhill and pool in low-lying hollows. A tree planted on a rise may be ten degrees warmer on a cold winter night than another tree, just yards away downhill. If frosts do come, orange grove owners often try to protect their trees by lighting small wood bonfires or oil heaters ("smudge pots") to warm the air.

Groves of oranges and other citrus fruits were originally grown from seedlings. But there are a number of disadvantages in raising these fruit trees from seedlings. Usually the seedlings are thorny, and they grow into tall, slender trees that are hard to pick. (They eventually fill out after about twenty years.) They may take up to ten years to begin bearing. And even more important, orange seeds do not always breed true. The orange trees that grow from them may not be like their parents at all. Imagine planting the seeds of a delicious orange, caring for the young trees for ten years, and then discovering that the oranges they bear are not as tasty as you expected!

Fortunately there are ways to propagate orange trees and other fruit trees and obtain young trees exactly like the parents. The most popular method for oranges and other citrus crops is by budding.

The first step in growing budded orange trees is selecting the right rootstock, the hardy tree that will serve as the foundation. Sour orange stock is often used in wet, heavy soils. Trees grown on this stock bear early and produce fine-quality fruits. Sour orange stock can stand a great deal of waterlogging, and it is resistant to foot rot, a fungus disease that is readily spread in damp weather. (Sweet orange stock is rarely used in Florida any more because of its susceptibility to foot rot.) But sour orange stock has

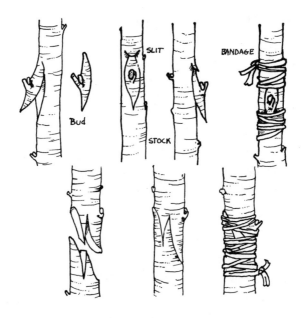

some important disadvantages. It has low resistance to a killing virus disease, tristeza, transmitted from tree to tree by insects. And it does not do well on light, sandy soils.

The operation of budding is quite simple. First the rootstock is grown from a seed until its stem is about the thickness of a pencil. (This takes about four to six months when the growing conditions are good.) Then a bud is cut from a branch of a mature orange tree of the right variety. A cut shaped like an upside-down T is made in the bark of the rootstock, about three or four inches from the ground. The flaps of bark are gently pried up with the point of a knife, and the bud is slid into the slit on the root-stock. The wound is wrapped around and around snugly like a mummy, with strips of cloth, plastic, rubber, or string. (Gummed tape is not used, because it might injure the bud when it is removed.) The wrappings are left in place for about three weeks. Then it is time to unwrap the bud and see if the operation was a success. If the bud is green, all is well. Then the bud is forced to sprout by cutting the rootstock partway through a little above the bud union, or cutting the top off entirely. The bud sprouts and grows and puts out leaves. The new top of the young tree, called the scion, is tied loosely to a stake so that it will grow up strong and straight. Once it is full grown, the scar of the bud union—the place where the scion and rootstock were joined—will show only as a faint line around the trunk of the tree.

Budded orange trees are usually lower and more compactly built than seedling trees. Eventually they reach a height of twenty to thirty feet, and their branches spread to a diameter of about thirty feet if they are not crowded. They begin bearing sooner than seedling trees—usually a few fruits in the fourth year, and then a good yield in the fifth. The oranges they bear are of the same variety as the tree from which the bud was taken, but there may be some differences in the smoothness and thickness of the peel, the amount of juice, and the amounts of sugar and vitamins, depending on the rootstock that was used, the kind of soil, and the weather conditions. In fact, orange growers know that there are great variations in the taste and aroma of oranges not only depending on where they are planted, but even differences among oranges on the same tree. Fruit that can be reached from the ground is not as sweet as the fruit that grows high up on the tree. Fruit from the outside of the tree is sweeter than inside fruit, growing closer to the trunk. The oranges growing on the south side of a tree are the sweetest, while those on the north side have the least sugar, and also less juice and vitamin C. In fact, even in a single orange there are variations—from segment to segment, and from one end to another. (The blossom end is sweeter and juicier than the stem end.) The next time you eat an orange, see if you can taste any differences among the different parts.

Orange trees bloom in the spring and summer, and they ripen in about eight to fifteen months, depending on the variety of orange and on the weather. They need heat to ripen, and in hot regions can ripen in the fall and winter months. But in cooler climates, oranges usually ripen at least a year after the trees have bloomed. In the late spring, an orange tree may be carrying last year's fruit, now almost ripe, blossoms, and young green fruits, all at the same time.

Orange blossoms, like most flowers, contain the plant's sex organs, both male and female. In the center is a single pistil, the female organ. The pistil of a flower looks very much like a vase, with a slender neck and a broad, rounded base. Inside the lower part of the pistil, called the ovary, are the ovules or eggs that can develop into seeds. The pistils of orange blossoms, like those of other citrus plants, are divided into a number of segments called carpels, each of which may contain one or more ovules.

Around the pistil are the stamens, each shaped something like a long slender stalk with a ball on top. The stamens carry the pollen, the male cells of the blossom. If pollen falls on the top of the pistil, each pollen grain begins to sprout. Its tiny tube grows down the neck of the pistil and into the ovary, where a pollen cell may join with an ovule and fertilize it. The pollen from one blossom may fall upon its own pistil. Or insect visitors, such as bees, may carry pollen from one blossom to another, perhaps from one tree to another. The fertilized ovule develops into a seed, and the walls of the ovary develop into a fleshy fruit. But as in many other fruit trees, orange blossoms do not need to be pollinated in order to develop into fruits.

It is curious to think that scientists consider oranges to be berries. By this they mean that the orange is a simple fleshy fruit, which develops from a single ovary. (Grapes and tomatoes are also berries.) As the young orange grows, the carpels develop into the individual segments, which come apart easily when the fruit is eaten. The walls of the ovary develop into the rind, with its spongy white inner layer (the albedo) and its colored, waxy-coated outer layer (the flavedo), as well as the tough membranes that wrap the individual segments. Running down the center of the fruit is a soft axis of pith. Inside each orange segment are hundreds of tiny juice sacs, which contain water, sugars, citric acids, salts, and vitamins.

At first the young orange fruits are quite green. The green color comes from the green pigment chlorophyll in the outer part of the rind. The chlorophyll in the flavedo of young oranges is the same pigment that is found in the leaves of plants. It serves them as a kind of energy trap, which takes in and holds some of the energy of sunlight. It does not absorb the green rays, though, and it is the reflected green light that we see. Using the energy absorbed by chlorophyll, plants are able to put together carbon dioxide, a gas from the air, and water from the soil, and manufacture sugars and other complicated chemicals from these simple raw materials.

Even though they look green, young oranges also contain orange pigments called carotenoids. Their color is masked by the green chlorophyll. The peel of the oranges also contains an enzyme called chloro-phyllase. This is a chemical that can break down chlorophyll. In the young oranges the chlorophyll is protected from chlorophyllase by a thin membrane called a tonoplast. Cool temperatures make the tonoplasts in orange peel break down, and then the enzyme reacts with chlorophyll and destroys it. With the green pigment gone, the carotenoids can be seen, and the orange acquires an orange color. The best temperature for turning oranges orange is about 40°F. In some parts of the world, such as Thailand, even the nights never get cool enough to make oranges turn color. The oranges eaten by Thais are as green as grass. In California's San Joaquin Valley, cool air from the snow-covered Sierras sweeps down each night, bringing the temperature close to freezing, and the oranges turn a beautiful bright orange. In Florida orange country, particularly in the autumn, the nights do not get cool enough, and the early-season oranges are often greenish, even though they are fully ripe. The late-season Valencias turn orange before they are entirely ripe and then produce more chlorophyll and turn green again by the time they are ready to be picked. Housewives shopping at the supermarket often pass them by, and yet orange growers say that late-season Valencias are the finest oranges of all.

Orange trees make an attractive and useful addition to yards and gardens in the warm regions of the world. But by far the majority of orange trees are planted in huge commercial orange groves, which stretch out as far as the eye can see.

ORANGES IN THE MARKETPLACE

Orange growing today is big business. In the state of Florida alone, there are already more than sixty million citrus trees in groves covering nearly a million acres, and most of them are orange varieties. More than a hundred million gallons of frozen concentrated orange juice is produced each year.

In some ways, the big orange grower cares for his orange trees in much the same way as the small homeowner with an orange tree in his backyard. He propagates trees by budding and follows a regular program of applying fertilizers at certain times of the year, particularly on sandy soil. But the large grower uses machinery for many tasks that the small gardener must do by hand. Mechanical cultivators go up and down the rows of trees, removing weeds. Keeping the ground under citrus trees clear of weed

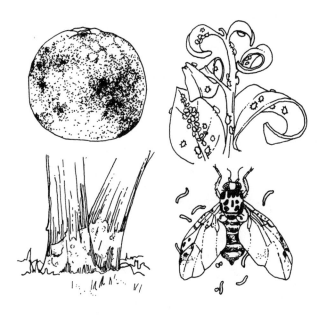

growth is important for two reasons: first of all, grass and other ground cover takes up part of the fertilizer that should be used by the tree; more important, tall weeds would block the flow of cold air along the ground and prevent it from draining down away from the groves.

Pruning machines also patrol the groves, trimming the trees when necessary. Spraying of fertilizer mixtures and pesticides is also mechanized. Whenever many plants of one kind are grown together, as happens in most types of modern agriculture, pests and diseases find it much easier to spread. Orange growers must cope with a variety of pests and diseases. Aphids, mites, and scale insects can damage leaves and fruits. Aphids can also transmit the virus that causes tristeza, or quick decline, which kills citrus trees quickly. Melanose and foot rot are fungus diseases. Melanose kills leaves and spoils fruit, while foot rot affects the roots and lower trunks of trees and can eventually kill them. The spreading decline is a disease caused by burrowing roundworms, which attack the roots of the tree as deep as fourteen feet below the surface. So far, the only really effective method of control for this disease is to bulldoze and burn all the infested trees, fumigate the soil, and leave it fallow for two years. It is easy to see why this citrus plague has already cost growers millions of dollars.

At the borders of the United States, inspectors are constantly on the alert to prevent Mediterranean fruit flies from slipping into the country. Already there have been several narrow escapes, and orange growers dread the thought of a full-scale invasion of this pest. The Mediterranean fruit fly is a fruit spoiler. It lays its eggs in the peel of citrus fruits, and the larvae burrow into the pulp.

Various methods are used in the fight against citrus pests and diseases. Resistant varieties of plants are bred and used wherever possible. The life cycles of pests are being studied thoroughly, and natural enemies—both predators and parasites—have been discovered and used against them. A complicated program of pesticide spraying is also used. Care is taken to use sprays that will evaporate or break down into harmless substances before the oranges are picked. For by law, the outer peel of oranges must be as wholesome and safe to eat as the inner pulp.

With all the mechanization of orange growing, so far there is one operation that must still be done by human beings—picking the harvest. Not that there has been any lack of trying to find mechanical ways to pick oranges! Giant mechanical combs have been tried, as well as mechanical tree shakers. Another machine, basically a system of huge air blowers has one drawback: it tends to blow the leaves off the trees along with the oranges. The problem is complicated by the fact that for many orange varieties each tree is bearing not only ripe oranges, but also blossoms and young green fruit that will form the next year's crop. So far, no really satisfactory mechanical substitute for the human picker has been invented. But this is still an active area of research, for there is a growing shortage of orange pickers, and soon there may not be enough to pick the whole crop.

Orange picking begins in the morning, as soon as the dew on the trees has dried. (When oranges are wet, their skin becomes taut, and they bruise easily. So they are never picked when they are still covered with dew.) The orange picker sets his ladder against the tree, then climbs up with a large bag slung over his shoulder. He picks the oranges within reach, either by snipping them off with metal clippers or by pulling them with a twist of the wrist. Pulling is much faster, but some varieties, such as tangerines, must be snipped because if they are twisted off, a plug of peel pulls out of the stem end of the fruit. When the bag is full, the orange picker opens it from the bottom and allows the fruit to roll out into a large field box. An average orange tree bears about fifteen hundred oranges, and it can be picked clean by an experienced picker in about an hour. Some trees have borne as many as twelve thousand oranges at one time.

Trucks carry the filled boxes to the packing house or processing plant. The treatment freshly picked oranges receive is quite different, depending on whether they are to be eating oranges or will be processed into concentrate. For many oranges that will be sold whole in grocery stores and supermarkets, the first stop is in the degreening room. Many consumers do not understand that green or green-spotted oranges can be perfectly ripe, and prefer to buy their oranges bright orange. Researchers have discovered a method for developing an orange color in the peels of the fruits whose chlorophyll has not been destroyed by exposure to cool weather. They treat the oranges with a gas called ethylene oxide. This gas causes the tonoplasts in the peel to relax and no longer protect the chlorophyll. The oranges are quickly "degreened." (Perhaps you are wondering why the packers do not simply put the oranges in the refrigerator until they turn orange. Unfortunately, the membranes no longer react to cold after the fruits are picked.) The use of ethylene oxide gas on oranges seems at first thought to be rather unnatural. Yet many fruits, such as bananas and apples, actually give off ethylene oxide, and if they are stacked in the same room with green oranges will cause them to turn color.

Another method of getting oranges orange is to dye them. The use of dye on oranges is strictly regulated by law. California does not permit it at all. In Florida only one dye, Citrus Red No. 2, may be used. Dyed oranges must be stamped "color added," and they must have at least 10 percent more juice than undyed oranges. Of course, the dye affects only the outside of the peel, and does not penetrate into the inner part of the orange.

Before the oranges are packed, they are first washed and scrubbed with hot soapy water, rinsed, and dried. Then a thin layer of wax is painted onto the outside of the peel. The wax used is an edible one, and it replaces the coating of natural wax that is removed when the oranges are cleaned. Without their coating of wax, oranges would breathe too rapidly and would quickly shrivel. For like other fruits, oranges continue to live for some time after they have been picked. One thing that oranges do not do, however, is ripen after they are picked. Many fruits do— for weeks after picking their stored starch is gradually converted to sugar, and they grow riper and riper. But oranges and other citrus fruits have no stored starch, only sugars. They must ripen on the tree or not at all, and the law requires that only fully ripened oranges can be picked and sold. (The next time you see an ad for "tree-ripened oranges," you will know that it was written for people who do not know very much about oranges—since all the oranges sold have been tree-ripened.)

The washed and waxed oranges pass along a conveyor belt, while workers take out

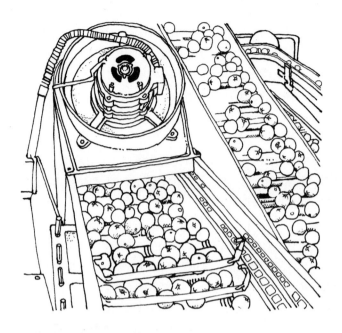

any damaged ones, grade the oranges for size, and pack them into boxes, cartons, or mesh bags. The workers wear gloves to avoid accidentally scratching the oranges with a fingernail. Even the slightest scratch might be an entry point for molds that could spoil the oranges before they reach the table.

Oranges destined for orange juice are sent directly to the cannery, where they are washed and squeezed by automatic machines. The juice is separated from the pulp and from the oils, and then placed in cans of various sizes. Canned orange juice is sterilized by pasteurizing, just like milk. The process kills germs but does not affect the vitamin C that the juice contains.

In the 1945-46 season, there was a revolution in the orange juice industry. For the first time, frozen concentrated orange juice was produced on a commercial scale. Production is relatively simple: most of the water is removed from the juice by evacuation under vacuum at low temperatures. The idea was not new in 1945—many people had discovered long before that it is easy to concentrate orange juice. The only trouble was that the evaporation process also removed various compounds that give orange juice its taste. Finally an answer was found by Dr. Louis Gardner MacDowell, a researcher at the Florida Citrus Commission. His answer was dramatically simple and effective: to superconcentrate the juice and then add a little fresh juice to it, along with some flavor essences and peel oil. This idea seemed so simple that at first the U.S. Patent Office refused to grant a patent for it. But as the production of concentrate by this "cutback" method quickly zoomed up into the millions of gallons, a patent was granted to Dr. MacDowell and his associates, who turned it over to the Secretary of Agriculture for free use by the people of the United States.

Orange processing leaves a mountain of pulp and other by-products, but these do

not go to waste. The pulp, peel, and seeds are ground with a bit of lime and turned into a nutritious feed for livestock. (An alert agricultural researcher got the idea for that use when he noticed cattle feeding on discarded fruit.) Orange peel cattle feed helps produce a glossy coat and thick, high-quality flesh.

Oil of orange, obtained from the peel, is used as a flavoring agent. It is also used in paints and varnish, to harden rubber, and as an essence for perfumes. Orange seeds yield a polyunsaturated oil that can be processed into a salad oil. The albedo of the peel yields a jelling substance called pectin and a group of compounds called flavonoids, which work with vitamin C to reduce fragility of blood capillaries and are used by doctors to treat various diseases. Waste juices can be used to produce ethyl alcohol. Table wines are produced from orange juices, and the peels of oranges are often candied, dried, or made into marmalade.

Other parts of the orange tree are also used commercially. Oil of orange is only one of three different essential oils that the orange tree yields. Oil of petitgrain, obtained from orange leaves and twigs, is used in making perfume. Oil of neroli, squeezed out of orange blossoms, is used in flavorings and perfumes. Orange blossoms are also used indirectly in the production of orange blossom honey. Bees gather nectar from the orange blossoms and turn it into a delicious honey that holds some of the delicate fragrance of the blossoms.

49

ORANGES AND THE FUTURE

Today's scientists are eagerly studying a number of chemical substances found in oranges and searching for new ways to use them. Meanwhile, agricultural researchers are constantly at work, trying to breed new varieties that will be more resistant to cold and diseases, easier to pick, and with interesting new taste qualities.

The success of Temple oranges, tangelos, and other citrus hybrids provides a great incentive to searches for promising new varieties. Crossing citrus varieties, and even citrus plants of different species, is easy to accomplish because the blossoms are readily cross-pollinated. But researchers run into an unusual problem when they try to breed citrus hybrids in this way. In addition to the embryo plants that result from cross-fertilization, citrus seeds often develop what is called nucellar embryos, which are exactly like their mother plant, with none of the characteristics of the plant that produced the pollen. The young seedlings that develop from such nucellar embryos are usually more vigorous than the hybrid embryos. So a researcher trying to cross-breed two citrus species usually winds up with a large number of pure-bred seedlings and only a few of the hybrids he is looking for. But citrus seedlings look very much alike. Often it cannot be told by looking at them what kind of tree they will grow into until they actually grow up into trees and begin bearing fruit. Citrus breeding thus can be a very frustrating quest, stretching over many years and requiring an enormous amount of space. Fortunately, chemical tests have been developed that can identify whether seedlings are hybrids while they are still very young. Using such tests, the researcher no longer has to grow hundreds of trees in hopes of discovering a few promising hybrids.

One of the main objects of present-day citrus research is to devise mechanical methods for picking oranges and other citrus fruits. Some of the devices already invented are suitable for picking fruits to be processed into concentrates, but they cause too much damage to be used for eating fruits.

Another important subject of study is the effect of air pollution and other aspects of modern life on citrus crops. Florida, California, and other orange-growing regions are becoming ever more industrialized. As people flock in, one orange grove after another is giving way to housing developments and factory complexes. New orange groves often must be located on lands that have poorer soil, and new varieties must be bred for the new conditions. In addition, industrial factories emit pollutants such as fluorine into the air. Researchers at the Citrus Experiment Station in Lake Alfred, Florida, have found that fluorine pollution produces a mottling of the citrus foliage, and sometimes causes the leaves to fall and the trees to be weakened. Now they are trying to determine what can be done about such effects.

Oranges and other citrus fruits have long been prized for the high content of vitamin C. It has since been found that vitamin C is a relatively simple compound, called ascorbic acid. It can be mass-produced, readily and cheaply, from simple industrial raw materials. Although it is much more pleasant to get your daily vitamin C from an orange or a glass of orange juice, people are increasingly relying on vitamin pills.

Modern research on the medical benefits of oranges and other citrus fruits has been concentrated on a more complicated group of chemicals called flavonoids. The main flavonoid in oranges is a substance called hesperidin. (Remember the golden apples of the Hesperides!) It is found in the fruits, blossoms, leaves, twigs, and bark of various citrus species. In orange fruits, most of the hesperidin is found in the albedo, the spongy inner part of the rind, as well as in the central pith and in the fibrous membranes that enclose the individual segments. Medical researchers have found that hesperidin improves the permeability of the blood capillaries (their ability to allow gases and water to pass through their thin walls) and helps to make them less fragile. Hesperidin and related substances have been found effective in preventing threatened miscarriages and various other conditions in which a tendency for bleeding is a problem. Some researchers say that citrus flavonoids work with vitamin C to help prevent common colds and make cold symptoms less severe. Indeed, the list of diseases against which hesperidin has been used reads like a medical catalog, including such items as asthma, beriberi, bursitis, diabetes, influenza, leprosy, measles, polio, rheumatic fever, stroke, and tuberculosis. Many of these treatments are still controversial, and there is also some argument as to whether these flavonoids should be considered as vitamins (they were originally named vitamin P, but that name is not usually used any longer) or as drugs.

Another interesting line of research on hesperidin and other citrus flavonoids is the search for artificial sweetening agents. Dieters were upset in 1969, when the Federal Food and Drug Administration banned cyclamate, a commonly used artificial sweetening agent, because it had been found to cause cancer in experimental animals, in addition to various other disturbing effects in other laboratory tests. Later studies indicating that saccharin, the other widely used artificial sweetener, may also be dangerous have further sparked a frantic search for safe substitutes. The flavonoids found in citrus peels have surprisingly proved to be a promising source of such compounds.

When frozen orange juice concentrate is manufactured, hesperidin often appears as a scale on the evaporator. If it is dissolved in acetic acid (the substance that gives the characteristic odor to vinegar) and then crystals are allowed to form, hesperidin forms fine, shiny colorless needles in a beautiful rosette pattern. Dissolved in water, it is tasteless, although many related flavonoids such as neohesperidin (found in the peels of Seville oranges) and narangen (from grapefruit peels) are quite bitter. Yet scientists have found that when these flavonoids are chemically changed slightly, they become sweet—far sweeter than sugar. One form, neohesperidin dihydrochalcone, for example, is 1,500 times as sweet as ordinary table sugar. If tests show that these new sweeteners are safe, perhaps not too far in the future you will be reading their names on the labels of soft drinks, canned desserts, and a variety of other food products.

FUN WITH ORANGES

EXPERIMENTING WITH ORANGES

There are some desert plants whose seeds come to life only after a rare rainfall. The seeds sprout, draw in the precious moisture as they grow rapidly, bloom, form new seeds, and die—all within a few weeks. Oranges could never win a race with such speedy growers as these. Their motto is "slow and steady." An orange grower must wait for years until his young trees begin to bear. Indeed, a great deal of patience is needed just to wait for orange seeds to sprout. We planted a few orange seeds in a pot, watered them regularly, and waited four whole weeks before a single shoot poked up out of the ground. It grew slowly, unfurled a leaf and then another, as we continued to give it water and sun. Then, when the young shoot was already a month old, two more sprouts suddenly poked up out of the soil—nearly two months after the seeds were planted.

So you will need patience if you want to have fun with oranges by planting their seeds. But if you do have the patience, you can learn a great deal about oranges and other plants as well.

For example, plant the seeds of several different kinds of oranges. Label each pot, and then see if you can notice any differences. Do they all sprout in the same time? Are the leaves all the same color and shape? Do they have the same number and arrangement of leaves? Do some grow faster than others? When do their stems turn woody? Plant some lemon and grapefruit seeds, too, and compare the seedlings with orange seedlings.

Some orange varieties grow best in certain kinds of soils. Try planting orange seeds in different kinds of soils—very sandy soil, red clay soil, and rich black soil. Compare oranges of different varieties. Which grows best in each type of soil?

Plants manufacture their own food. They take in water from the soil and a gas called carbon dioxide from the air. Using the energy of sunlight, they put these simple chemicals together like building blocks to form sugars and other complicated chemicals. Scientists call this process *photosynthesis.*

How much water do orange seedlings need to grow? Plant seeds of the same variety in several pots. After they sprout, try giving each pot a different amount of water. Keep the soil in one pot wet all the time. Let the soil in another pot dry out thoroughly each time before you water it again. Give another pot a moderate supply of water. Measure out the amount of water you add to each pot, and keep records of how much and how often you water each pot. Which orange seedlings grow best? Carefully dig up one seedling from each pot and examine the roots. Which seedling has the most roots? Which has the longest roots? (Often plants that grow in areas that receive a lot of rainfall tend to have shallow roots, while plants that grow in drier climates have deeper roots.)

How much sunlight do orange seedlings need? Try giving a group of seedlings in pots different amounts of light each day—two hours for one pot, four for another, six, eight, ten, twelve, and so on, all the way up to a full twenty-four hours a day. You can regulate the amount of light the plants receive by leaving them on a sunny windowsill for a certain number of hours each day, then moving the pots to a shaded place. For the pots that are to receive more hours of sunlight than the windowsill receives, add an artificial light for the needed number of extra hours. (Plants grow best in a combination of both a fluorescent light and an incandescent bulb. The combination is closer to real sunlight than either type alone.)

What would happen if you placed an orange seedling in a dark closet, where it received no light at all? You would find that it turned a pale yellowish color. It cannot make its green pigment, chlorophyll, without sunlight. And without chlorophyll, it cannot manufacture its own food, for the pigment helps to capture the sunlight energy in plant leaves. If you left the seedling in the dark closet long enough, it would die, even if it had enough water. But what would happen if you placed such a yellowed seedling in the light?

Light is so important to plants that they can even turn their leaves and bend their stems so that the largest possible leaf surface is exposed to the light. If you lightly feel the leaves and stems of an orange seedling, they seem very stiff and firm. It seems hard to imagine them moving. Yet a movie made by time-lapse photography would show the leaves of an orange tree turning to follow the sun as its position in the sky changes from morning to evening. Scientists call this kind of reaction *phototropism*, which literally means "light turning."

Observe your orange seedlings at various times of the day. Are the leaves turned toward the sunny window during the day? Try turning the pot around so that the leaves are facing away from the sun, then look at the seedlings every ten minutes. How long does it take them to turn their leaves toward the sun again?

Although plants make their own food, they do need some nourishment from the soil. Plant some orange seeds in pots of clean sand. Water one pot with distilled (pure) water. Water another with mineral water. Water still another with a solution of a commercial fertilizer in water. Which seedlings grow best. Do any of them grow as well as orange seedlings planted in soil?

Some people say that talking to plants or playing music in the room where they are kept can help or hinder their growth. Some researchers have even tried hooking up a lie detector machine to plants, and they claim that plants show one kind of reaction when people water them or do other things for them, and a different kind of reaction when someone cuts off a branch or burns a leaf. They claim that plants even react when people *think* good or bad thoughts about them. This whole field is still very controversial just now—many scientists feel that all these claims are nonsense, or that the effects can be explained in other ways. For example, talking to plants may help them to grow because of the carbon dioxide the gardener breathes on them when he talks. You might try talking to your plants, or playing different kinds of music to them, and see if they respond. Perhaps you can make a contribution to our knowledge of the world around us.

ORANGES FOR GOOD EATING

What is the best way to eat an orange? Your answer will depend not only on your personal taste, but to some degree on where you live. The oranges Australian children carry to school with them are usually peeled in a spiral halfway down, with the peel replaced around the fruit like a wrapper. When it is time to eat the orange, the child unwinds the peel and holds the fruit like an ice-cream cone. Norwegian children like to take off the top of an orange, make a hole in the pulp,

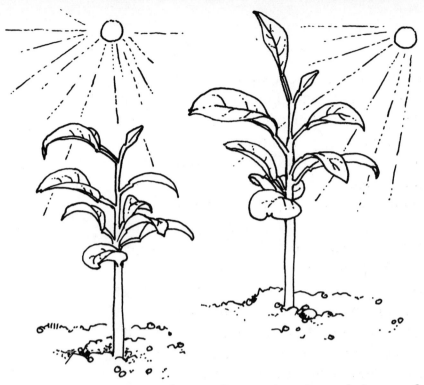

insert a lump of sugar into it, and then suck the orange juice through the sugar lump. In Nepal, people usually prefer to eat oranges cut into quarters, pulling the juicy pulp away from the peel as they eat. In Switzerland, sometimes orange segments are served topped with sugar and whipped cream.

Probably most of the oranges eaten in the United States are either eaten fresh in the hand, or drunk as juice—hand-squeezed, canned, or prepared from concentrate. Either way, they are a fine source of vitamins —especially vitamin C—minerals, and quick-energy sugars. Oranges and orange juice should be eaten as fresh as possible, for when they are exposed to air some of their vitamin C gradually breaks down. Storing in a refrigerator helps to slow this breakdown. Canned orange juice and frozen concentrate keep their vitamin C content through long storage periods. But as soon as the can is opened and the juice is exposed to air, it must be treated just like fresh orange juice.

How can you tell whether the oranges you see in the store will be good eating? Look for firm, heavy oranges with fresh, bright-looking skin. Lightweight oranges are likely to be rather dry and tasteless inside. Very rough skin means that the skin is unusually thick—with less juicy flesh inside. (Of course, you must make allowances for the variety of orange, since some types normally have a thicker, rougher skin than others.) Dull, dry skin with a spongy texture tells you that the oranges are getting old, and will not be very good eating. Stay away from oranges with cuts or punctures in the skin, soft spots, and discolored, weakened areas at the ends —they are probably decayed. But don't worry about green spots. They do not mean the oranges are unripe, for all the oranges that are picked commercially are fully ripened right on the tree. (Before the oranges in a grove are picked, an inspector takes samples and runs tests to make sure they are really ripe.) A brown or blackish speckling over the skin also is not usually anything to worry about. It is called "russeting," and it is often found on oranges from Florida and Texas. It does not affect the eating quality of an orange; in fact, russeting often occurs on the best-quality eating oranges, with a very thin skin. But remember one thing: when you are picking oranges—or any fruit—from a supermarket or grocery store display, handle them gently. If you bruise or cut a fruit and then put it back, some other person is going to get a damaged fruit. Or perhaps no one will buy it, and the store owner will have to throw it away. You will end up paying for such spoilage indirectly, through higher prices for the fruit you buy.

Although oranges and orange juice are good eating by themselves, they can also be used with other foods to make many tasty and interesting dishes.

Take salads, for example. Orange segments are often mixed with grapefruit segments and other fruits such as strawberries, blueberries, melon balls, and grapes to make delicious fruit cups. Arrange orange segments like sunbeams on a large lettuce leaf and add a mound of cottage cheese in the middle for another attractive and nutritious salad. Or combine oranges with other vegetables and fruits. For example, try this variation:

Carrot, Orange, Raisin, and Peanut Salad

    1½ cups finely chopped carrot
    1½ cups diced orange
    ½ cup raisins
    ½ cup salad dressing
    ½ cup chopped peanuts

All the ingredients should be cold. Toss the carrots, oranges, and raisins together lightly with two forks, adding enough salad dressing to moisten. Serve on lettuce and sprinkle with peanuts. Makes six servings.

Orange fruit cups are good for desserts, too. To add a festive feeling, you might sprinkle a topping of shredded coconut onto each serving. But if you'd like something even sweeter, you might try one of these orange dessert recipes:

Orange Custard

    2 cups milk
    2 eggs, beaten
    1 cup sugar
    2 tablespoons cornstarch
    1 teaspoon butter
    ⅛ teaspoon salt
    2 tablespoons lime juice
    6 oranges, sectioned

Mix the sugar and cornstarch and add cold milk. Add the beaten eggs. Cook over hot water in a double boiler until the mixture thickens. Remove from heat. Add butter, salt, and lime juice. Cool. Place the orange sections in sherbet glasses. Pour the custard over them and top with whipped cream. Makes six servings.

Orange Snow

1 tablespoon gelatin
¼ cup cold water
¼ cup hot water
¼ cup sugar
¼ teaspoon salt
1 cup orange juice
3 medium oranges, sectioned
1 tablespoon lime juice
2 egg whites, beaten until stiff

Soften the gelatin in cold water. Add hot water and stir until dissolved. Add sugar, salt, fruit juices, and orange sections cut into small pieces; mix thoroughly. Cool. When the mixture starts to thicken, beat until frothy. Fold in stiffly beaten egg whites. Turn into a mold that has been rinsed in cold water. Chill until firm. Unmold and garnish with orange slices and strawberries. Makes six servings.

Orange Pecan Cookies

    1½ cups shortening
    ¾ cup brown sugar
    ¾ cup granulated sugar
    1 large egg, unbeaten
    ¾ cup chopped nuts
    ¼ cup grated orange rind
    ¼ cup orange juice
    4 cups flour, plus 2 tablespoons
    ¼ teaspoon soda
    ¼ teaspoon salt

Combine shortening and sugar. Add egg, salt, grated rind, and juice. Beat well. Sift soda and flour together. Add to the mixture and blend well. Add nuts. Shape into rolls 2 inches across. Wrap in waxed paper and chill several hours. Slice ¼ inch thick. Bake at 400°F, 8 to 10 minutes. Makes 5 dozen cookies.

You can make a number of delicious variations of orange cakes and orange breads by adding grated orange peel and substituting orange juice for part of the liquid in cake and bread mixes, or in your favorite cake or bread recipe. Orange flavor adds something special to chiffon cakes, muffins, and nut breads.

Would you like to try something different for breakfast? Perhaps orange French toast or orange fritters will be just the thing to perk up your early-morning appetite.

Orange French Toast

                    1 egg
                    ¼ cup orange juice
                    1 teaspoon lemon juice
                    ¼ cup granulated sugar
                    1½ teaspoons grated orange rind
                    3 slices bread
                       butter or margarine
                    2 oranges, sliced or sectioned
                       powdered sugar

Beat egg. Add orange and lemon juice and beat again. Add sugar and grated orange rind; mix thoroughly. Cut slices of bread in half or in any shape desired. Dip in egg mixture. Fry in butter or margarine until golden brown. Place orange slices or sections on each slice of toast. Sprinkle with powdered sugar. Serve at once. Makes two servings.

Orange Fritters

                    2 medium-sized oranges, peeled,
                       sliced ¼ inch thick and
                       sprinkled with sugar
                    1 egg, beaten well
                    ¼ cup milk
                    ½ tablespoon melted butter
                    ½ cup sifted flour
                    ½ teaspoon baking powder
                    1 teaspoon sugar
                    ¼ teaspoon salt

Mix beaten egg, milk, and melted butter. Sift flour, baking powder, sugar, and salt together. Stir into liquid. Dip orange slices in batter. Fry in deep fat at medium temperature. Serve with orange syrup, made from ¼ cup orange juice concentrate, ¼ cup butter, and 1 cup maple syrup. Makes four servings.

Try a little orange butter on your toast. To prepare it, soften one stick of butter or margarine and mix in 2 tablespoons of sugar and 2 tablespoons finely grated orange rind. Then chill to harden again and serve. Other tasty spreads can be made by blending 2 tablespoons of orange juice concentrate with 3 ounces cream cheese, or ¼ cup orange juice concentrate with ¼ cup peanut butter. Beat until smooth.

Or perhaps you'd like to make your own orange marmalade. Oranges are particularly good for making marmalades and jellies because they are rich in acid and pectin, a natural jelling substance.

Orange Marmalade

Wash 6 oranges. Quarter and remove seeds. Put through a food chopper. Then measure the ground fruit. Add three cups of water for each cup of pulp. Bring to a boil and cook covered for 15 minutes. Let stand overnight. This is the stock for making marmalade.

When the stock is ready, measure out 3 cups of stock into a large heavy saucepan. Add ½ cup lemon or lime juice. Measure out 3 cups of sugar. Bring the stock to a boil. Add sugar, stir to dissolve, and cook rapidly, stirring from time to time until a jelly or candy thermometer reaches 220°F. Remove from heat and let cool to 190°F. (The cooling is to prevent bits of peel from floating to the top.) Pour into clean jars with airtight lids. Seal at once.

Orange juice makes a delicious beverage, not only by itself, but also mixed with other fruit juices, such as apple, cranberry, grape, grapefruit, pineapple, prune, and apricot juices. For a nourishing between-meals snack or a party drink, try orange eggnog:

Orange Eggnog

1 egg, separated
2 tablespoons sugar
½ cup milk
1 cup orange juice

The orange juice and milk should be cold. Beat the egg yolk until light and fluffy. Beat the egg white until stiff, but not dry, adding the sugar gradually. Combine egg yolk and white, and stir in the milk and orange juice. Makes two servings.

You can also use orange juice to pep up main dishes. Prepare beets, carrots, squash, or sweet potatoes with a glaze made from orange juice concentrate mixed with brown sugar or honey, butter, and a bit of nutmeg. Or try an orange sauce on baked luncheon meats, ham, pork, or chicken.

Orange Sauce with Raisins

> ½ cup brown sugar
> 1 tablespoon cornstarch
> ½ cup boiling water
> ½ cup orange juice
>   grated rind of 1 orange
> 2 tablespoons lemon juice
> ½ cup raisins

Mix the sugar and cornstarch. Add boiling water and boil for 5 minutes. Cool and add the orange juice, orange rind, lemon juice, and raisins. Serve over meat or over desserts such as puddings, custards, or ice cream.

Many of these recipes, along with many more delicious ways of fixing citrus fruits, are found in a series of circulars, "Using Florida Citrus Fruits," prepared by the University of Florida Agricultural Extension Service in Gainesville, Florida. You can get free copies of them by writing to the Dade County Agricultural and Home Economics Department, 2690 N.W. Seventh Avenue, Miami, Fla. 33127.

ORANGE GAMES
AND CRAFTS

In the fifteenth century in Breslau, a city that is now part of Poland but was once part of Germany, there was an annual orange shoot. Marksmen took turns shooting oranges off one another's heads. During the same century, there was a legend in Switzerland about a hero, William Tell, who was forced to shoot an apple off his son's head with an arrow. William Tell never really existed; perhaps the legend had its beginnings in stories of travelers returning from Breslau, but then the fruit was changed from an orange to an apple in the telling and retelling.

Shooting oranges off people's heads may have been considered fun in the fifteenth century, but it is *not* an activity we recommend! But there are many, safer ways you can have fun with oranges.

You can make cheerful orange "people" by drawing eyes, nose, and mouth on an orange with nontoxic marker pens or tempera paints. Add a paper hat and a stiff cardboard collar to serve as a stand. If you eat the oranges later, be sure to throw away the peel. Or you may save your orange people for a while by spraying the orange with a lacquer spray or painting it with shellac.

An orange is also just the right size to make a head for a hand puppet. Carefully cut a circle about an inch and a half in diameter around the top of an orange and scoop out the pulp without breaking or tearing the rind. Then turn the hollow orange rind over with the hole underneath and paint a face on it. Make a cloth dress or robe large enough to cover your hand, and pin the neck to the orange "head" in several places along the opening.

At Halloween an orange makes a fine miniature jack o'lantern. Paint the features on with black nontoxic marker, or carve them out with a knife. Be careful to cut off only the outer, colored part of the rind (the flavedo), leaving the spongy white albedo showing through underneath.

Children in England use oranges in a different way at Halloween. They make orange-peel "false teeth" and wedge them over their gums to give themselves a properly monstrous look.

Soon after oranges were introduced into Europe, these golden fruits became a favorite Christmas gift and an important part of the holiday decorations and celebrations. In Germany, the holiday season began on the eve of December 6, when Saint Nicholas and his elf, Knecht Ruppricht, brought gifts of oranges, cookies, and toys for the children. Children in Switzerland put their shoes on the kitchen hearth on Christmas eve and found them stuffed with oranges, nuts, and sweetmeats in the morning.

In Italy, the *Ceppo* was a center of Christmas celebration. This was a Nativity scene, gaily decorated with oranges, candy, and toys. *Ceppi* were sold already decorated, but without the presents. Sometimes families had one *Ceppo* for each child. The parents and friends secretly added the oranges, sweets, and toys to surprise the children on Christmas day.

You can build your own *Ceppo* this Christmas, with plywood shelves and wooden dowel supports. Use bright red and green paint for the shelves and supports. Decorate them with burlap or yarn braids and raffia flowers, for a real Italian look. And don't forget the oranges!

Popular party games that are normally played with apples or potatoes can also be played with oranges. For example, bob for oranges instead of apples. Or try to pass an orange along a line of people, while each of you touches the orange only with your nose and forehead, without using your hands.

An orange is round like a globe, so if you draw the outlines of the continents on an orange and carefully pare away the flavedo from the parts corresponding to the oceans and lakes, you will have a miniature map of the world.

On side streets in New York and other cities, children play a game called Bottle Caps or "Skully." A large board is drawn on the sidewalk or street with chalk, with a skull in the middle and the numbers from 1 to 12 arranged around it. Each player in turn squats down next to the playing board (when there are no cars coming!) and flicks a soda bottle cap with a tap of his finger. If his cap lands in one of the numbered boxes, he adds that number to his score. (The skull counts

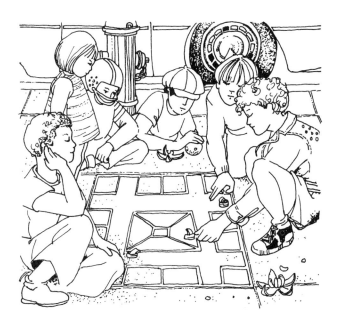

as 13.) You can make a skully board for yourself on a large piece of cardboard. If you try your hand at this game, you will find, just as generations of city children have discovered, that a piece of orange peel wedged into the bottle cap gives it just the right weight and balance for shooting.

You can make an attractive printed design with oranges. Cut an orange in half, across its long axis, and leave it out overnight to dry. Then smear the cut surface with colored ink and press onto a piece of paper or cloth. When the orange dries, the juicy parts tend to sink in, while the dividers between the segments and other fibers stay firm; to-

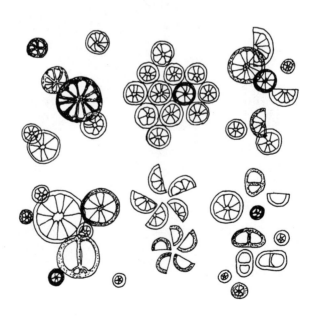

gether with the rind, they form the outline that is transferred to the paper or cloth. You can get artistic effects by using several different-sized oranges (or slices at different levels from the same orange), different-colored inks, and by the way you space the orange prints.

In medieval times, people often carried a pomander to protect them from infection. This was a ball of perfumes, placed in a perforated bag or box, and hung around the person's neck with a ribbon or chain. No one believes any more that perfumes can protect you from disease, but a pomander can give a pleasant spicy odor to your closets or drawers. Here's how to make one:

You'll need a fresh orange, a box of whole cloves, powdered orris root, ground cinnamon, and a ribbon. (You should be able to get the orris root from a drugstore. If you can't, you can leave it out.)

Use an awl or an icepick to carefully prick holes over the outside of the orange, and stick a whole clove in each hole until the orange is completely covered. Then roll the orange in a mixture (half-and-half) of orris root and ground cinnamon. Pat in as much powder as will stick to the orange. Then wrap the pomander in tissue paper and leave it for several weeks. After that, remove the paper, shake off any loose powder, and attach a ribbon around it so that you can hang it up.

You can play games with orange seeds. Save up the seeds from oranges you eat until you have about two dozen. Then dye the seeds with vegetable coloring or tempera paint—some red, some blue, some green, some yellow.

Here is one simple game that two or more can play with the colored seeds: Take two seeds of each color. Shake the eight seeds in your hand, then toss them onto a tabletop or the floor or sidewalk. You get a point each time a pair of seeds of the same color land close together. Each player takes his turn, and the game is continued for ten rounds. The player with the most points wins.

For another game, make an 8-inch circle on a piece of cardboard and color it in red, blue, yellow and green segments. Take one seed of each color, shake them, and toss them down onto the board. Any seed that lands on a segment of the same color scores points according to the following values:

Blue—blue	1 point
Yellow—yellow	5 points
Green—green	10 points
Red—red	25 points

You can probably think of more

games to play with the colored orange seeds.

Before you eat an orange, guess how much it weighs. Take a guess from everyone around, and then weigh the orange and see who was closest. Before long, you will be pretty good at "sizing up" an orange just by looking at it. Are some varieties of oranges heavier than others? With two oranges of about the same size, which weighs more, one with a thick rind or one with a thin rind? Try guessing how much the rind will weigh, and then weigh the orange after you peel it.

As a variation, try guessing the weights in grams. In recent years, there has been a great deal of discussion about switching over to the metric system. The United States is the last large country that still uses ounces and pounds, inches and feet, and other "English" measures. Having a different system from the rest of the world is making us lose a lot of world trade. But many people are reluctant to make the change, because they are so used to figuring weights and measures the old way that they cannot think in meters and grams. By guessing the weights of oranges in grams, you can help yourself to become familiar with the metric system.

You can even make a game out of eating oranges. Our children made up these contests:

Count the number of seeds in your orange. Whoever has the most seeds wins. (Only whole seeds count. No fair biting a seed in half while the other person isn't looking.)

Peel the orange as carefully as you can, trying to get the peel off in one single strip. The person whose peel comes off in the smallest number of pieces wins. (Using a knife is not allowed.)

If you squeeze your own orange juice, each take an orange and see who can squeeze out the most juice. (Your mother should be happy to see you playing this game.)

Think about it the next time you eat an orange. Probably you can think up some more games and contests yourself.

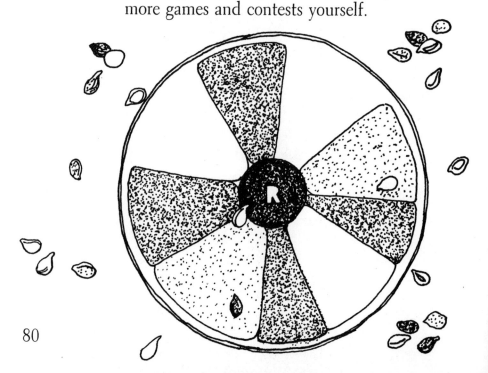

BIBLIOGRAPHY

General
McPhee, John. *Oranges*. Farrar, Straus and Giroux, New York, 1966.

Florida Department of Agriculture. *The Story of Florida Citrus*. Bulletin No. 177, June 1969.

Growing Oranges
Soule, James, and Lawrence, Fred P. *How to Grow Your Own Citrus Trees*. Florida Cooperative Extension Service, Institute of Food and Agricultural Sciences, University of Florida, Gainesville. Circular 339.

Lawrence, Fred P. *Citrus Fruit for the Dooryard*. Institute of Food and Agricultural Sciences, Agricultural Extension Service, University of Florida, Gainesville. Bulletin 166C, May 1969.

Orange Recipes
Use Florida Citrus Fruits Around the Clock. Institutional and Educational Department, Florida Department of Citrus, Lakeland, Florida.

25 Ways to Use Frozen Florida Orange Juice Concentrate. Department of Information, Florida Citrus Commission, 551 Fifth Avenue, New York, N.Y. 10017.

Marmalades, Jellies and Preserves. Florida Cooperative Extension Scrvice, University of Florida, Institute of Food and Agricultural Sciences, Gainesville. Extension Home Economics Bulletin No. 137.

Using Florida Citrus Fruits: a series of circulars prepared by the Agricultural Extension Service, University of Florida, Gainesville, including:

Circular 229, Citrus Salads
Circular 230, Citrus Beverages
Circular 231, Citrus Desserts and Cookies
Circular 232, Citrus Breads
Circular 233, Citrus Pies and Cookies
Circular 234, Citrus Garnishes and
   Seasonings
Circular 236, Canning and Freezing Citrus

Homemaker's Citrus Recipe Kit For Oranges, Lemons, Grapefruit, Tangerines, and Limes: a packet of recipe leaflets available free from Sunkist Growers, Inc., Consumer Service, P.O. Box 7888, Valley Annex, Van Nuys, California 91409.

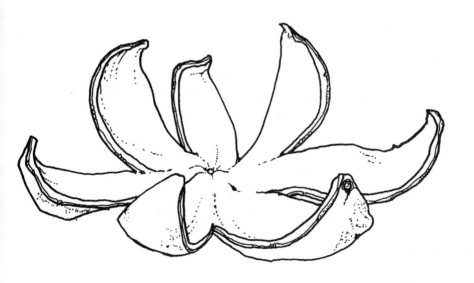

INDEX

Vitamin *P*. *See* flavonoids.

Western Hemisphere, spread of oranges
    to, 7
Witchcraft, oranges in, 16–17
Wolfskill oranges, 9, 10
Wolfskill, William, 8–10